dear future self

AN ANTHOLOGY TO INSPIRE SELF-CONFIDENCE

BY SUSAN LOWENTHAL AXELROD

Dear Future Self:
An Anthology to Inspire Self-Confidence

ISBN: 979-8-218-10574-7

First Edition - November 2022

Published by JGU Press. Printed in the USA.

Design & Layout by Carasmatic Design - www.CarasmaticDesign.com

CONTENTS

PREFACE

*"Progress or regress? Life got too busy, too chaotic; too much. Leaders reduced to power-mongering, workers stressed beyond human limits, families stretched beyond patience and love, children over-scheduled and burdened into obesity, depression, even suicide. The richest in the world lived high and kept it to themselves while the poorest died in the streets. Religious leaders abused their flocks, organized religion crumbled. Human sensibility dimmed and the earth suffered."**

Is this written about modern-day or pre-1789 France? Were we actually in the best of times? Are we in the worst of times, yet? From nearly the beginning of recorded time, there is evidence of gain and loss, strength and weakness, hubris and humility. Will there ever be a time in human history when this is not so? Perhaps, if in the future humans become genetically integrated with robotic circuits that dull emotions and create a false sense of 'stable' mental outlook. Until that time, with incalculable passion we rail, we cry, we shout and fight, we laugh and we love. Until that time, we emote from the deepest place of power we were given, the Soul.

*Original composition by author Susan L. Axelrod

What is happening in the world today? Is it an 'unseen foe,' lack of preparation and selfish leadership by those in power, or a long, slow decline of concern about humanity and the earth? Looking for an enemy is the human response, blaming others for everything is the go-to for most. 'Not my fault' becomes 'not my problem' and as such, Soul, the greatest concern of all that is, suffers and sinks into the darkest recesses of consciousness. When the Soul is shuddering and shuttered, the human vessel is then permitted to live as it wants, in self-orientation, with total lack of consideration for the greater good of humanity and for our earth. And darkness reigns. Then, sadness, depression, despair, anxiety, and fear propel up, out and swirl around each human and throughout the universe.

But There is Light

If you can catch your breath, quiet your mind, and open your eyes, then you can see the beauty still around you. It's in the earth that our Mother renews annually in spring. It's in the human race that the Divine deems worthy to continue no matter what. It's in the stories of the mundane, of one person reaching out to another, of a child's delight, of an elder sharing wisdom with a younger. Of humans connecting over the internet checking in with relationships formerly forgotten or neglected.

An Entreaty for All Time

Ask yourself the still-relevant age-old entreaty: "If I am not for myself, who will be for me?" (on self-care, putting on your oxygen mask first). "If I am only for myself, what am I?" (on consideration of humanity and taking action). "And if not now, when?" (the original nod to mindfulness, being present). [Rabbi Hillel, c. 110 BCE–10 CE]

And this question I devised for myself and now share out in the world, an entreaty for our time: "Who do I want to be and how do I want to be; what can I do?" This simple question asked over and over by humans throughout the world can help turn on the light that dispels darkness. It is the ultimate control. Each one of us taking personal responsibility for humanity and the earth. Activate your brain by asking that simple question; activate your heart by taking action and you will fuel your Soul's Rise. As Soul rises, growing light will dispel the darkness. Start with loving yourself more, move quickly from self to other, love others without judgment, find faith and community that supports and you will feel rejoined with humanity; being the light that is needed in our time.

INTRODUCTION

Confidently Designing Life

Dear Reader,

"I wish I knew then what I know now."

This phrase is so common that it's not even source-cited anywhere. It sure resonates though, doesn't it? "I wish I knew then what I know now"...Have you ever thought it?

But, but, but, what if you did know something now that would support you then? Is that too mind-bending to grasp? It used to be for me. In my former Type-A self, things were linear, straight and narrow, up or down/ back or forth, no grey for me. The masculine energy of logic and action was firmly entrenched in my psyche, the feminine energy of flow and nurture, nowhere to be found. I blamed 'time' for it all, one of my favorite excuses. I never had time to 'be' because I was always 'doing.' And, in the too-much-doing, there was never enough (money, energy, agency).

Now, I've coined it enoughness. When I was young,

ambitious, a wife, momma, worker, volunteer, daughter and daughter-in-law, sister, friend, dog owner, community member and good citizen, there was just never enough time. That's how it felt all the time for me. ...I wish I knew then what I know now...

But what if you could speak to your future self? What if you could tell her that you have learned there is enough? If you could speak to your future self, what would you tell her?

I speak to my Future Self frequently now. I tell her that I'm living in abundance to provide for her, taking care of her physical body, tending to her mental and emotional health, growing daily to support her spiritual health, and staying focused on purposefulness to sustain flexibility and freedom to live as I want...easily supporting self, women and girls who are the future mommas of the world.

You? What would you tell your future self?

Wishing you the best always,

Susan

NOTE: I hope you will read all the way through to the end of this book where you will find Dear Future Self quotes from a dozen other women. They are thoughtful, insightful and inspiring! Then, you will have an opportunity to write your own Dear Future Self thoughts from all you've gleaned and gained throughout your experience of this book. Have fun with it!

1

STARING INTO THE UNKNOWN

What do you see when you look ahead? Do you see a clear path, straight and narrow with all the familiar plans you seeded and cultivated for years? Or, are you in a transition-due to your own making or not-where you look out ahead and all you see is an untrod, unshorn and unfamiliar path? What happened to that carefully laid plan? Do you ask yourself, "How did this happen? How am I suddenly unsure of my next step?" Are you frantically looking back to see where you went wrong, what you can take back or do differently to keep things the same? Are you surfing vertiginous waves attempting balance without success? Or, if you are one of the lucky ones to simply be in a natural transition, do you even still feel unsettled inside? Fret not, this is your Soul beginning to move again.

Suppressed or even shut down for years-by our parents, society, school, marriages or partnerships, business, community, religion and more, the women's soul submerges for self-protection or at least shelter in the torrents that overwhelm the early open, loving, sweet-natured, innocent countenance of girl-children. Each trauma, vast or slight, moves a soul deeper and deeper in self-protection. She stays there, shuddering and shuttered, until the opportunity arises for her to look up and peek out and she begins to stretch and move.

For women who have developed a trusting and sacred sisterhood along the way in the first half of life, the freeing of the soul can be felt when in concert with that corps. Inevitably, though, when she moves back into her traditional daily space, the soul plunges again; sometimes free-falling or sometimes gently settling back into that deeper space of shelter. Whether faced with extreme personal difficulty in marriage or business, or simply marginal boredom of life's sameness, as a woman comes into her second half, her soul begins to move.

This may manifest in nerves, pain, unease, or simply a bit of discomfort. By the time women hit maturity and independence—'the second half'—the soul has often been still for a long time. As a woman ages, the soul awakens again. She stretches to peek out, muscles expand and contract, dulled nerve fibers become sensitive and activated. But for the wisdom gleaned and

The soul awakens.

gained through all her life's experiences, she might wince or wilt. Instead, the soul excitedly knows: 'It's my turn now.' And she rises.

self-reflections

2

STEP BY STEP

As a young professional, I did everything quickly. Famous for the tap, tap, tap of my high heels walking quickly down the hallways at work, I walked with intention; I was a leader and I was in charge. These lessons learned in leadership development programs in high school became controlling thoughts on my middle journey. But the purposefulness turned into just hurrying as I moved through those maturing adult years, executing on the expected in the life of an ivy-educated upper middle class, married working mother (or ANY woman). Get married, buy a house, have a family, volunteer and always do more, more, more. Doing more is one of the perpetrated patriarchal messages that have been part of a downfall for the soul of women. Whether a woman loved homemaking or moved into a paying career (where she never gave up the many jobs embedded at home), the 'faster now in heels' message applied as television steered a mad voyage of obsessed consumerism, with Madison Avenue as the rudder.

I didn't know it then, but while hurrying through my life, my soul started sinking lower and lower down in me. The 'being' space of heart and soul became subsumed to the 'doing' space of mind and body. I created a wonderful, beautiful life, but I was rushing through it unconsciously. Doing more and more of what was 'expected' left me lacking in the intentionality of heartfelt purposefulness. I forgot the passion of youthful exuberance and got sucked into the whirlpool of mental and physical expectations. My voyage simply stopped dead one normal day-at-the-office in an emotional overwhelm that ended up lasting for 10 days, resulting in loss of peripheral vision and total bed-ridden incapacity. Eventually, I got my vision back and found a new life-normal on medication working with a psychiatrist who helped me cross the bridge from human-doing to human-being. That was an eye-opener with an extraordinary view from the other side. As I learned to 'just be' more with permission to do less, I shiftcd to a feeling-state from a thinking-state. Later, I went into different therapy to deal with the fear of aging and found someone trained in soul consciousness, which turned my perspective-shift into a life-shift.

One of my greatest awakenings was the connection between my physical body and my mental state/

New–to–me information poured forth.

mindset. New-to-me information poured forth as I made a conscious effort (after seven years) to get off medication while maintaining a commitment to mindful living. When my doctor told me, "If you want to get off medication, get yourself to the gym," I did. And began a healthier, more purposeful journey-of-my-lifetime. I have stayed off medication by connecting my soul with my mind and body in infinite alignment, showing up daily as who and how I want 'to be' in mindfully present awareness of the impact I am intended to make. I still walk briskly (good for my body!) but now my hurrying is on-purpose and for the benefit of the world.

self-reflections

3

IS SHE OUT THERE?

Is she out there? Or, is she in us? That perfect woman, wife, worker, the Wonderwoman of our minds. Isn't she who we have aspired to be? Isn't she the vision we have grown up with, the vision on the screen, emblazoned on our brains from the vulnerable age of impression? She was untouchable, unabashed, and unbounded by the human constraints that we saw in our grandmothers, mothers, and aunties. When we thought about the woman we would become, was she not supposed to be unassailable? She was.

But it was not just we, the children, who pulled her in from the screen that became one with our brains, it was also the mothers of the day watching her and saying, *I wish I could be like her. I wish I could have those superpowers.* And the men in their lives, latently developing expectations of their wives; and the boys who would grow up to become men in power, still in charge in the Patriarchy of today. And the mothers and fathers of that day who lived in latency of unrequited desire imposed it on their children. We are those children. The unrequited desire of being a wonder woman is now in us.

But what if we see a "wonder" woman differently? What if the power of her was seared into our brains, not just the picture of her? What if the wonder is of the earth, of the miracles, of the blessings and angels that surround us if we see them? What if the power of 'wonder' is that and not the picture of physical beauty, strength, and invincibility? What if love, gentleness, and calm confidence are the true powers, the powers in us that make us more than merely mortal; the powers in us that live beyond the time and space of our physical beings?

When you meet up with your future self, do you want to be beaten and battered from the Struggle and Fight? Or do you want to be healthy, whole, soul-connected and ethereal to best support the rest of her journey? Whether the Future Self is in the near or far universe, how do you want to best support her? It is important to ask this question now; indeed, her best well-being depends on coming to consciousness of this question. The answer to this question is the place of wonder, of power, of your control over your destiny. It

What if love, gentleness, and calm confidence are the true powers?

informs your thoughts, actions, beliefs, and Soul intention for this moment, and this one, and this one...

Living in the moment, one moment at a time, in a well-being frame of mind, makes you the Wonder woman of today and tomorrow.

self-reflections

4

QUALITY ALONE TIME SERVES YOUR SOUL

Equanimity: "Mental calmness, composure, and evenness of temper, especially in a difficult situation." After living my first few decades in the antonyms of equanimity—restlessness, disquiet, impatience, and discomposure—I was relieved to get on the path to a better place, an easier way of being through equanimity. Finding my center by discovering my breath was the biggest step toward a future I could only begin to imagine. I had lived with negative or hyperbolic thoughts running wild and attacking my nervous system, stoking depression or anxiety with relentless sway. I had no tools to ward it all off; they didn't teach that in school. And, at least among my forebears, matriarchs of prior generations were not afforded the luxury of getting 'zen' to hand down to me.

I'm grateful beyond compare to have found authors, mentors, coaches, and a therapist to guide my journey. These teachers offered their instruments which I adopted and adapted for my own use, making it all work in a way that allowed me to get soul-connected and calm. And I had family and friends who supported me, allowing me to grow beyond the burden of rigid legacy or societal strictures that I railed against, loving me no matter what. Oh, but don't think I haven't been challenged since! To be human is to be challenged with life's impositions. Darkness, sadness, betrayal, confusion, terror, angst, and fear. For some, these burdens visit with devastating regularity. I'm grateful to have found equanimity on my own journey and I created tools to address the challenges.

In addition to breathing, stretching and mindset transformation tools, I learned that quality alone time is vital to my wellbeing. I say 'quality' alone time because I don't mean mindless enervating time spent on devices when not in my impact space. I love my social media time when I'm thoughtfully seeing what people are saying or needing and being able to respond in a supportive, positive or inspired way. I feel uplifted doing this work and countless people have personally messaged thanks for what I share. But the other times, mindlessly surfing, scrolling, or unconsciously watching inane shows, this actually depletes me and does not serve.

Small bits of alone time offers plenty of opportunity for soul-connection.

Quality alone time includes doing anything out in nature! Being in partnership with Mother Nature and God soothes my soul and sparks my imagination. Two decades ago, I learned to voice dictate what came to my mind and those thoughts turned into speeches, articles, and eventually, original guided meditations came forth from that quality time outside. Other examples of quality alone time include resting, reading, writing, exercising, and beading, a hobby I love.

What about you, do you have quality alone time? If so, how does it serve? If not, what can you do to figure it out? It does not have to be hours at a time. Like small bits of exercise cumulate to make excellent physical impact, small bits of alone time offers plenty of opportunity for soul-connection. Do it now; don't wait.

self-reflections

5

WHAT IS YOUR TRUEST TRUTH?

When the bells and whistles quiet down, when your mind-circus closes for the night, you have the best opportunity to stand in your truth. Your truest truth. IF you can face it. Truth: 'that which is true in accordance with fact or reality.' What do you do with that opportunity?

During the day, everything pulls, regular life activities toll, notifications ding incessantly, responsibilities nag and thoughts pop up like whack-a-moles. How do you respond? When noise surrounds you, it's easy to allow falsehoods to prevail. You tell yourself this and you tell yourself that about how you are feeling based on the thoughts that ruminate from the noise. The thoughts give rise to words that you say out loud. You hear your own words. And, from the noise in your head that rings in your ears, you give yourself permission to believe. Permission to hear the words you are speaking as truth. But are they? Your truth? Or, do you feel tormented by what you are thinking, saying, sharing? Do you feel besieged by fraud, at best, or by full deceit, at worst? And, if by some chance these thoughts and words rise to what you consider truth, there is further to rise. To your truest truth. To the truth in you that eases your heart and comforts your soul.

When the mind-circus shuts down for the night, how do you feel? Have you been true to yourself, to your heart, to your soul? When you are laying in bed at night, can you feel yourself standing tall in your truest truth? Or, do you feel small in your inner knowing, the knowing that only you have, that you've told lies; that you've been untrue to those you love and to yourself?

Can you face your future self, square on, look right in her eyes and say to her, "I spoke the truth"? Try it, see how you feel. If your answer to yourself is "No, I can't, I simply can't look her in the eyes," then think; and think more. How can you quiet the noise, purify your thoughts, feel and live in your truest truth and rise up to the highest point to share it with others? What will it take?

Try believing in yourself, your core, your soul. What if you are getting life right? Exactly as it is, exactly as you are doing it? What if you can be true

Try believing in yourself, your core, your soul.

to yourself, share your truest truth with others AND feel soul-connected? Use the opportunity nightly, when the mind-circus shuts down to tell yourself, "I'm getting it right." "I'm ok." "I'm in my truest truth." And, a new pattern will emerge: you, in truth. In your truest truth. Then, you can look your future self in the eyes and say, "I stood in my truth for you."

self-reflections

6

YOUR FUTURE HOLDS SURPRISES

It feels like you spend most of your life getting set up and situated for the things you have been told to expect. Year after year you go to school, you do the work that is required. Perhaps you move directly on to college or start your career after high school. And shortly thereafter you begin thinking about the family that society says you should create. While we are fortunate to live in this time where the makeup of the family doesn't look the way it always did in the past, there is still much pressure to conform. Following the path of generations that came before us, doing what we are told, doing what is needed to live a 'life,' the life our ancestors brought us to. We hold responsibility to that life, but the hold it has on us can create ties that bind. Then, along the way of living life, you come to expect that things will go as you have planned them.

But inevitably, things do not go as planned. Often if not always, as you get older, you get smacked upside the head with something huge that went awry. If you're lucky, it's not a mortal illness. Though, to keep it real, the betrayal that women experience can feel like a mortal illness, whether from career trauma, an affair, addiction, apathy, or dementia onset that might have been delayed if the partner had tended to their mental, emotional, and physical wellness. As we get older, naturally we experience more of real-life that includes these betrayals, and illness, loss, deep sorrow, and mind-altering grief. Sometimes, too much to even bear. When life's course is suddenly altered, it's a sobering, even shocking experience. But what if we were ready for it?

What if, instead of being taken down in a swirl of anxious overwhelm, you take a stand now? A stand for yourself, for your emotional wellbeing and for your mental stability... what if you create a well-orientation to life that offers a foundation of rock, sturdy beneath your feet? Platelets will shift, without a doubt, but the foundation will hold. What if the you of today thinks of your future self, the one who will otherwise suffer the consequences of holding-in years, or even decades, of worry, anxiety, or fear? What if, today, you tend to mindfulness, purposefulness, physical outlet, and

What if the you of today thinks of your future self?

emotional processing? What if you get resources in place and your thoughts in good order so that you are more ready to handle what life inevitably throws at you?

It is possible, IF you face your future with open mind and heart, and understand the opportunity of taking responsibility for your Self. That is what brings life into your control, proactively considering what you personally need to get shored up inside; figuring it out for yourself, and doing what it takes to be strong physically, mentally, emotionally and spiritually. Your future will hold surprises, you can count on that. How you handle them is up to you.

self-reflections

UP AND DOWNS CREATE RICHNESS

Are we intended to experience only one feeling? Are we intended to be in a calm and happy place all the time? If you were, how would you know it? Contrast serves the richest life. How can you know joy if you know only joy? But what of the hard times that face us? What of the obstacles, struggles, and personal challenges? What of them? Why do they seem to come at us with frequency and force?

Why is it that just at the time you feel you have things in order, the next step breaks under your weight? Why is it that when you finally feel things are in your control and going the way you've always wanted, that a storm kicks up, tossing things around, drenching and drowning the things that you have grown?

Part of the answer is enlightenment. Enlightenment doesn't come from nothing, it comes from overcoming anything; struggle, dissonance, conflict, darkness. Think of the hardest thing you've ever overcome. Give yourself permission to look full on, deep into that space you were in. When you were in that hardship, did you ever imagine that there would be a time again that you would see the light, that you would be able to breathe, to release, or just to Be?

I offer a shared human experience. There may be nothing harder than growing up as a child, every single day, facing an unknown world, everything ahead of you to learn. Everything is a question, "How does that work; how do I do that? Am I getting it right?" Yet, here you are today, somehow by a miracle, a functional adult. Think of another time, a hardship you faced. You got through that 'time,' that 'difficulty,' perhaps even that terrible place that you thought you would never live through. Yet, here you are breathing and living well in this time and place. This can be the greatest showing for yourself. You did that. Perhaps you had help, but it was still you who got yourself to here, where you are now.

And consider this: Enlightenment can be your friend. Seeking the light, even the tiniest point of light, illuminates the darkness. You have an opportunity to seek out any point of light. And then another, and another. Light each one of those candles from the one

Seeking the light, even the tiniest point of light, illuminates the darkness.

before it and you will see that the flame from the first does not diminish in any way, but the light overall grows brighter.

That is enough. But if you want more in your life, then become a point of light for another. And another. And another. And the tapestry of a rich life will be woven. Your life, richer than you ever imagined. Your currency, good will, calm, love and even joy. Yours, from the experiences you've overcome, the challenges you've conquered and the mountains you climbed. The ups and downs create the richness of life.

self-reflections

8

THE SHARED EXPERIENCE: COVID-19

As chaos reigned throughout the world during the early days of the Pandemic of 2020, there was one thing we could hold onto in nearly physical reality, the shared experience of crushing disappointment. Every soul experienced some sort of crushing disappointment as the pandemic rolled in. Plans for both normal life and special times shut down in a supernatural way, almost as if there was a big switch in the sky being turned off by a source bigger than humanity itself.

No event was too sacred, not weddings, funerals, graduations or major sports/arts/cultural events; not vacations, nor professional conferences. And events that were formerly considered mundane became elevated to a new level of conscious commitment by mortals on earth. Golf and tennis games, walks with friends, book clubs, religious services, regular business, dinner out, grandparent visits, going to the park, getting your nails done–each of these activities previously just the 'stuff' of normal life when we lived in the glossy haze of all that was.

And when we lost it all, there was crushing disappointment. Whose was worse? Was it the bride with her white dress fitted and ready for the altar? Was it the family of the patriarch, who died alone buried in front of a camera lens? Was it the student missing out on the rites of passage of her senior year or the college graduate losing the job that was going to start his 'real life'? Was it the new restaurateur ready to launch with the opening that would never be? Or, was it the PTA dad who had planned the Spring father-daughter dance that never happened? Crushing disappointments, all.

Like the shared experience of crushing disappointments, there was the shared experience of fear of the virus of our time, COVID-19. The days of fear, before treatment, before a vaccine, germs spreading unknowingly, deaths mushrooming in terrifying numbers; people sheltering in place, some poor, elderly, or new parents without items necessary to live. For generations, we had been looking for something to bring people together in shared harmony, something that transcended politics, religion, language,

Kindness touches the soul through love.

culture, and borders. As the fog of the Pandemic descended, it turned out to be fear that held us together like glue across the planet.

Then, there was a 'pause.' A world-wide pause. Nearly every industry shuttered or a mere shadow of its former glory. Across the world, people sheltered in place, cars off the road, smokestacks silent, chemicals and pesticides dormant in their drums. And, as if God was parting the seas once again, the sky and the water cleared. Unable to imagine such a parting previously in our time, we experienced it again during the great Pause. Bright blue skies, clear green waters, the sound of birds in the eerie urban quiet.

And then, there was kindness. The shared experience of crushing disappointment became the shared joy of kindness. People, as if seeing others clearly for a first time, reached out. Businesses made free offerings, families connected weekly online, people gave, shared, supported and just loved each other.

self-reflections

9

STEPPING OUT OF YOUR LIFE

What if you got a chance to step outside of your regular life? Would you? Would you take that chance? What would have to happen for you to do it? If you imagine it, what comes to your mind? What do you see? Where would you go? What would you do? Am I the only one who ever wondered about this? I think not. I think there are many women who wonder, or yes, even yearn for this freedom.

And then comes the guilt. The guilt about the children left behind, the husband whose lunches would not be made, the elderly parents not cared for, the dog not walked, the household chores not done, the business team that would not be nurtured. So many things we do that have created our own overwhelming state, such that when a question like this is asked, would you ever want to walk away from your life, your answer would be a resounding, 'Yes!'

I did this once. I walked away from my life for a month. It took something drastic happening in my life. Prior to that thing happening, I would never have seen the vision of truly being able to do it. What about this? What about that? What about the other thing? What about him, her, them? All this did come to my mind. Yet, this thing was so strong, so severe, I knew I had no choice but to leave my life as it was; not forever, but, for a time. Even if only for a short time. I knew I needed to get away, to take care of myself, to nurture my soul and to explore my mind.

I did. And the world did not fall apart, though, family and friends were unhappy that I chose to fly during the Pandemic of 2020. I took great care, even while also taking a risk. And, when I went away, to a safe and loving place, I felt an ease in a way I had not felt for a long time. I gave myself permission to rest, to do nothing or anything I wanted. I gave over my responsibilities to others, and I gave up my responsibilities in my work, just for a while. No one fell apart, my work did not end, and when I returned home, I arrived safely, in a better state of mind, with a commitment to my Soul, to myself, to my family and to our world.

Open your mind and imagine the possibilities. Engage!

This journey is not for everyone. I realize there are many—perhaps most—who are not able to do what I did. Still, there are ways to do it. Even if only in your mind, or for a half-day get-away for yourself. As women, the importance of this cannot be overstated. There is no substitute for this. It is vitally important for our personal health, welfare, and wellbeing which is ultimately what affects our world. I encourage you to consider. Open your mind and imagine the possibilities. Engage!

self-reflections

10

PERCEPTION AS A BASIS OF WELL-BEING

Could this be your year? The year you look up, see the light, and feel a shift, just a bit of energy that gently nudges you forward. The year you claim what is yours—responsibility for your life, your demeanor, and your countenance—and say 'Yes' ('I am,' 'I can,' 'I want it,' or 'I will'). Could this be the year you make the change that has been on your mind, sing the song/write the book/dance the dance that has been on your heart and create the momentum to move in the direction you want to go? Your Soul has likely been crying out to you in ways you might not imagine. For example, are things going surprisingly right for you? Or cryingly wrong? Has immunocompromised illness appeared? Have you had unexpected life-losses or life-windfalls? Has an old friend re-connected or has a friend moved on from you? Any or many of these might be nudges moving you forward without your realizing it and depending on how you perceive them.

Tuning in to the perception of things that happen to you can create well-being in your mind and can change the trajectory of your life. So much of what happens 'to' us is a result of what happens 'in' us. And, yes, so much of what happens in us stems from negative things that happened long ago that created micro-abrasions to our souls. The familiar term is micro-aggression, and we know now that these little cuts from life–from anyone who may be close to us or even from total strangers–create an actual soul-pathway to negative self-mindset. This may have been something said once, or something repeated but regardless, our young mind goes over and over it, and it can spiritually lead to an activated nervous system that keeps us from sleeping well, from feeling peaceful, from finding hope or positivity in the world around us and so much more.

I ask you, why wait? No matter when you are reading this challenge to your soul–whatever season of a year or of your life, if you come to awareness of how you perceive things, you can create change more quickly than you think. Consider how much well-being affects you, is it not true that when you feel better you do better? And, of course, when you feel worse, you feel that you do worse (read that again). It is your perception of how you, yourself, are that can change the way

The next moment is already your future.

things go for you (and read that again!). Create a good well-being consciousness whenever you can, however, you can; do whatever it takes. This is what will help you change more quickly than waiting for time to pass, waiting until after something coming up 'soon,' waiting until next year, or waiting until any time other than now. The next moment is already your future; move towards it with an open mindset and improved perception of your well-being. Your soul will thank you.

self-reflections

11

WHAT HAPPENS WHEN YOU BARE YOUR SOUL?

What happens when you bare your soul? Have you ever considered this? For most, it is simply too hard, too raw, too real. It is easier to let the soul sit shuttered or shuddering deep down inside, the darkness offering cover in avoidance of the pain or difficulty. Avoidance, when allowed to penetrate, leads to denial. And denial then, seeps into your consciousness, sitting there taking up valuable real estate where otherwise the mind might be working in a healthy way.

Denial could be seen as a form of self-protection, simply protecting your soul from feeling confused, worried, hurt, sad, anxious or scared. If something is just too much for the mind to consider in truth, then telling yourself small untruths can help. But do small untruths not grow to big lies that you tell yourself? Even if the 'lie' is simply to avoid? In this way, time also offers cover. The small untruths you tell yourself can just sit quietly, over time taking root in your soul consciousness. The root that sprouts in innocent soul-interest, grows over time with intentional self-protection. If you dare to self-reflect and self-discover, if you willingly go to the place of your deepest thoughts, what labyrinth will you see there?

As you read these words, from the safe vantage point of 'now,' might it be possible to go in, go deep, dig through the weeds that have grown over your deepest fears and begin to gently tug? If this is too hard for you to consider, spend time tilling your soul-soil through breathing, journaling, drumming, chanting, meditation, affirmations or mantras or other methods of clearing. After a time, you will find that the weeds come up far more easily than you might think. Deepest fears might give way to personal realization of your strength, conviction and abilities. The thing you buried so deeply earlier in your life, might-at this later stage-no longer be served by avoidance or denial. Quite the opposite. It is possible that if you use confidence-inducing tools of clearing and commitment to soul-self, you will be able to see and realize that hacking away at the thick roots now will serve a stronger, more beautiful future.

It is, simply, time. Bare your soul to yourself first.

Consider facing the specters from your past, seeing them as the weeds that are growing indiscriminately, destroying your conscious self and creating the unconscious being you have become. Is this who you want to be now? Is this who you are now? Is this the way you want to live the remainder of your life?

It is not too late. It is not too hard. It is not too scary. It is, simply, time. Bare your soul to yourself first. Find and use tools or resources that work for you such as writing, therapy, coaching, a safe group or an accountability community. Then, share your nurturing wisdom with others. And your Soul will dance and sing. light of impact.

self-reflections

12

THE FUTURE WILL THANK US

Are you feeling invisible? Are you feeling that your middle-aged self, your body, your face, even your mind are not valued by those around you, possibly even the people in your own family? I see this sentiment expressed repeatedly in social media discussion threads of large women's groups. I can see these groups have become a lifeline for many. A safe space to ask embarrassing questions, to share feelings and emotions about this time of life where, blessedly, judgment is usually limited, and love is often abundant. Also, I read endless comments from women in midlife feeling unvalued and unseen. In my work as a Confidence Coach for women in the second half of life, I hear similar sentiments.

After my experience supporting my 91-year-old father in rehabilitation at a nursing home, seeing people live out the end of their lives inert and unfulfilled, I just want to scream, "Women, stop complaining about being unseen and see yourself!" You are stellar in every way. You are vital, smart, and beyond the worry of others' opinions. You have skills and life experience to share and can impact our world in ways beyond your imagination. And, the stakes are high.

Stop complaining and get to work. Right now, the time is now. It is not hyperbole to say the stakes are higher than ever. The world is literally melting from climate change, and we are worried about not being seen by men when we walk into a car dealership? See yourself; value yourself more. Accept and embrace your unique value proposition as a woman who can nurture, manage, and accomplish. Isn't that exactly what you've done for decades? Accomplished more than you could have imagined, caring for self, families, pets, work, church, community, partners, parents, and more?!

See yourself for who you are, now; step outside your comfort zone if that's what it takes. Get clear and confident on your own skills and abilities and get to work as a volunteer. If you need paid work, get your resume in order, cross-train with others, get comfortable speaking your message, realize the transference of your skills, and confidently charge the value of your worth. What if we do this and persist,

See yourself for who you are, now.

no matter what? We have decades ahead of us to create change that is desperately needed for our children and grandchildren's healthy future.

What if we step outside of our comfort zone and *see ourselves* and stop waiting to be seen by anyone else? What if we come out from behind our curtains of shame because our bodies are expanding or our faces are wrinkled? What if we expose ourselves for the skills and talents we have, beyond the ability for others to understand? Let them underestimate us, let us stand up, see ourselves, get seen and heard, and fight for our children, for the earth, and for humanity. The Future will thank us.

self-reflections

13

YOUR FUTURE IS NOW

Do you sometimes wonder, 'What happened to my life?' Didn't you have plans about how it would go? Didn't you think that doing the right things would lead to the next phase in good order? Didn't you imagine a gentle rise over time into 'the golden years,' despite the doubtless ebb and flow of some of life's shock waves coming in and receding? Didn't you get it all done, on time, in pretty good order and even with some flourish? So how did you get here, to this unknown place, now?

How did you arrive at this place of questioning, of not knowing very well who you are, and no longer comfortable in your own skin? The answer is simple, it truly is. Life happened. That's it, no more. Life happened while you were doing you. When you take time to reflect deeply on who you were every day to become the you of now, were there not days that you were less than conscious, getting-it-done by rote, not feeling connected to anything at all? Were there not nights that you were sleepless with worry and fear, feeling utterly alone, terrified of the tides? How many times were like this for you? How often were you 'out of your mind,' going through the motions, faithless, groundless, and depleting?

If you are like any woman in history, your honest answer to yourself is, "a lot." It's likely no one taught you how and gave you permission to tend better to yourself than to everyone else. Without this, it's nearly impossible to break through the legacy of being nurturers and caregivers to get to the ultimate blessing of self-care.

But I ask you, what about now? Who could you be and how could you be if you take time for honest reflection? What if you clean your windows to your soul and see through them more clearly to get soul-connected and bring feeling, love, and joy back to your Self? If you're feeling depleted, depressed, and down, the windows to your soul can also show you a future in charge of You. Pray, create, get out into nature, sing—these are just a few of the windows you can open and look out of that will provide beautiful expansive vistas that will bring back awe.

What will you do with today?

But the choice is yours. You can stay stuck in marginalization, or you can break through and break out into a spirit of joy that will feed you for the rest of your days. Did you do the best you could throughout your early years? Yes or no, those days are past. What will you do with today? Can you simply stand again, on your own feet, feeling that ground supporting you? Can you use your voice to sing, your body to dance? Can you walk among the trees and pray for universal guidance, abundant self-love, and a future of feeling again? You can if you want. Your future is no longer off in the distance, your future is...now.

self-reflections

14

DEAR FUTURE SELF

ear future self, I love you. I can say this with all my heart because I've learned the power of saying this profound phrase with true meaning. In the life I've lived, your past, I've learned love. And while I'm speaking to you in the future, I know not when, still I am grounded, Here and Now. Being consciously aware of this moment (and this one, and this) is another lesson I've learned. While earlier in life, you and I suffered many anxious moments worrying about a future we couldn't know, it turns out the reality had lower lows then we could have imagined, no? Oh, but also highs! Feelings, thoughts, experiences we could not have foreseen, remember? This moment, here and now, speaking to you is one! In this moment, how could our young, worried, busy, angry or sad selves ever have imagined the peace and joy of knowing we would break through concrete to arrive at consciousness? And then break through consciousness to feel an open heart space through which we would connect to soul!

And that our rising soul selves would show us intuition! And deeper still, that Intuition would reveal a bridge to a time continuum of all that ever was, past and future, and that we would courageously curate and lead an army of soul sisters across that bridge! To this moment, when I meet up with you, an army of sisters behind me, coming to lift you off the ground if needed, to help you rise if that is needed, or to protect and defend you or work for you or with you in purpose. Or, if you are quite well, then we shall all simply have coffee together by a stream, or by a fire chatting meaningfully about life.

But make no mistake, whichever way we find you, we are always here, looking out for you. We are doing all we can-ALL we can-to be healthy and well, to be brave and strong and to be loving, kind, compassionate and gentle to ourselves. We commit to this, for the army of our own soul selves—every one of them created from every moment of living. And we commit to lead the soul sisterhood, every one of them invited into the army of change to do her own best bidding in her own authentic way.

Find your own authentic voice.

And this final lesson, in this moment, in case you happen to need a gentle reminder: find your own authentic voice, she will be the one thing your Soul can hear. If it happens that your Soul is suffering and hiding, speak to her with your authentic voice, and she will be soothed. She will rise and she will shine again and lead the army of her own past souls and the army of the soul sisterhood! Open-hearted with ease and joy, dancing across a future bridge, divined and ordained. We, all of us, stand behind you, fully devoted to your future Self, in love.

self-reflections

15

ON THE BRINK

Can you feel it? Can you feel being at the edge, on the brink of something? Perhaps, a cliff? Does it feel as if your toes are hanging just over the edge? When you look out in front of you, do you see a colossal canyon that feels like a chasm opening up or waiting to swallow you in its vastness? Not in death, no, not in death, but in overwhelm, in consternation, agitation, or confusion? Or perhaps you feel like you are at the Ocean's Edge. Are your toes half on the sand with the water lapping over them teasingly threatening to pull you in; your heels digging in the sand to try to grab hold? For you, it may be a deep forest at dusk. Everywhere you turn there are shadows of trees that appear like the devil waiting to grab you and pull you over to the dark side. Every step you take, your foot lands on something that rustles or crackles making you cringe in worry or fear. On the brink, do you feel it?

What of it? Have you never been here before? Has there never been a time in your life that you awoke in sadness, overwhelm, or fear and went to sleep experiencing the same? There has. It may be before the time of your conscious memory, but surely you were in that space, the greatest void of all in front of you while in your mother's womb. Or, maybe more recently, during your life as a child, a young adult, in your adult years, or even recently in your mature years. And yet, here you are now; right now. Sitting, breathing, Being the perfect and unique creature, you are. Perhaps, a bit worse for wear, but the coat of patinaed feminine armor-shining, clean, unmarred in your innocence-is an honored testament to your battles hard fought and hard won.

And now, once again, you are on the brink, the vast valley in your line of sight. Is it another battle line drawn in front of you, a battle for our world? Nay, the battle for your soul. How will you gear up and rally, where will you go from the brink? Not pulling back-you've pulled back so many times before. This time, it will take a leap! How often have you heard the phrase, 'Leap and the net will appear!' Will it, though? Yes, it will! You see, you've been presetting the net since the day you were born, since the moment you chose to

Get clear
on who you
want to be
and how you
want to be!

bravely come forth into the greatest chasm of all-time, life. Each single step you've taken has landed you here, right here, right now. Come to conscious awareness of this, get clear on who you want to be and how you want to be! What is the purposeful impact you want to make in this world, at this time, on the brink? Leap, and know the net that catches you is the one you wove! This is your time.

self-reflections

Peace of Mind

This meditation can support your more confident Self. Peace of mind can be yours if you're willing to open to it, give yourself permission needed to break through the blocks, barriers or resistance to feeling better. Most of us are addicted to stress, it's simply the ocean we swim in now. Conscious awareness and mindful presence to this moment can support your move towards Peace of Mind. Meditation is one of the tools that can be game changing. Get into a quiet place where you can be uninterrupted for just ten minutes. Breathe, and read through this meditation to consciously create the way you want to feel.

What will it take for you to find peace of mind? Why is it so elusive? What will it take, what will it take, what will it take? Do you ask yourself this?

In our new world of soundbites and the way information is delivered to us, overwhelm is constant, peace of mind is elusive.

Often, we think it, we want it, we strive for it, but fall just short; peace of mind is elusive. Here is an answer, it may be The Answer; the answer you seek to the question that plagues you, "What will it take for me to find peace in my mind?" The Answer is breath, your breath; deep breath in, filling your lungs with oxygen that spreads through your body, charges your systems, circulates, expels, and repeats. Your Breath, the greatest tool in your kit to find peace of mind.

Let's take a breath here, a breath, the secret of life, the miracle of Life. Deep breath in and long breath out. And again, deep breath in and long breath out.

Do you suffer from having a mind filled with a lack of peace? When you commit to getting quiet, catching your breath and listening, just listening to what you find, is there chaos there? Or, if not chaos, maybe just overwhelm, worry, anxiety, sadness, or fear? Any measure of any of these feelings prevents Peace of Mind.

Is peace of mind necessary? Must we have peace of mind every day, all the time? Not per se, but yes, finding some measure of Peace of Mind daily will serve a best life, a confident life, life as you want it to be.

What will it take, what will it take, what will it take?

What is it that you want? How do you think peace of mind can serve? As you consider this question, use the secret of life, your breath, to help support your desire. Deep breath in and long breath out.

Why will peace of mind serve? Because your mind must be at peace in order to achieve that which you conceive.

Do you know what it is that you want? Do you desire wealth, glory, power? Are you sure this is what you want? Are you focused on it, then? Have you carefully conceived it? Or, are you instead in a wishing state? A frenetic state of mind that is clouded by doubts to your true success, by weak thoughts of "I can't," or "not for me," or "why not me?"

Is peace of mind necessary? Must we have peace of mind every day, all the time? Not per se, but yes, finding some measure of peace of mind daily will support you, it will lift you up; it will allow you to be inspired by what you desire, what you conceive and it will allow you to believe.

Believe what? That you can. You can find peace of mind, a quiet breath, a space of allowing, a calm countenance, even joy. Believe what? That you can be in charge, you can be in control of yourself, your thoughts, your feelings, your life. For this is what peace of mind means, just here, right here, in this moment; becoming aware, getting clear, feeling calm, and finding 'OK.' Just here, right here, in this moment, peace of mind.

CONCLUSION

Feeling Confident, Now What?

Dear Friend,

I started the introduction of this book with "Dear Reader."

Now, after our journey together through these pages, I call you Friend.

So, friend, now what? Live. Yes, live. Now that you know you can speak to your Future Self, you can spend less time worrying about her! After all, isn't that what we do? Spend so much time worrying about the next thing, or the thing after that, or turning the next decade age, or the new boss, or deterioration of mind or body, or the partner you want to find, or money and so much more.

Throughout these pages, if you have reflected and

connected with your future Self, you can feel more confident today. You can feel more in charge, more in control. You can speak to your next moment Self to assure her she will do ok (perfect is overrated!). You can speak to your next decade Self to let her know her pain will be gone because your now-Self is facing fears, getting active, learning tools and strategies to feel better and committing in a way your Younger Self did not. You can speak to your elderly Self to let her know she will be financially secure because your now-Self is no longer hiding and lying about money but rather she is learning and putting systems in place to shore up the accounts. And so on!

Can you feel that? Wow! Honestly, this is my thesis and even as I write these words in this letter to you, I can feel the confidence and power that comes from knowing I can DO this. I can make choices to take tiny steps or gigantic leaps-either way will get me to where I want to be in the future, no? Knowing your Self, in Soul-Connection, is what allows you to feel. And, friend, feeling is the basis of well-being. Coming into the feeling-state in our bodies allows our minds freedom to conceive. Being in the conceiving state in our minds allows our Souls freedom to rise. Being in the soul-rising state, well, that's where confidence lives.

Do you need to be in that high-confidence, soul-rising state every moment? Well, you can be if you want of course. But the truth of it all is that we're human first and as such, we fall and we fail and we suffer. Not to worry, though, contrast serves us. If you are in a perfect state-of-being all the time, you wouldn't know it because there would be no contrast in your life. Life's down moments now serve to help us feel more deeply life's up moments later. Can you see that?

Go ahead and connect with your Future Self. Let her know that you are doing what it takes today to support her through life's journey. Then, do that! Do what it takes today to support your Self through life's journey, in your control. You, in charge.

Please stay in touch.

With love,

Susan

'DEAR FUTURE SELF...'

As promised, here are quotes from a dozen other women to inspire your own Future Self journey:

Hang out with young people. "Young" does not refer to any particular age. An 85-year-old can be young, and a 45-year-old can be old. Young people are those who still have a zest for life and look forward to each new day. They will keep you young as well.
—*Judy Bloomberg, Always a Traveler, Never a Tourist*

Remember to have a kinder self-dialogue. You are worthy and deserve to be happy. Don't forget that there are people in the world that love you and appreciate you. You are not alone. Don't forget to embrace the loving moments and disregard the pettiness that sometimes steps forward. You are loved and you are worthy.
—*Susan Cohen*

Remember that you can be whatever you want to be. You have a voice, a mind, and a history to carry you forward. Stay active, stay engaged, give back to the community and always be open to trying and learning new things. Continue to grow...always and embrace your limits. Focus on the people you love since you now have more time and more resources and create new memories. Live in the moment, be present and enjoy your life!
—*Abigail Goldberg Spiegel*

You are stronger than you think and don't forget that what you are taken to, you will be taken through with love, grace, and dignity.
—Alina Haitz, www.AlinaRHaitz.com

You are strong enough, smart enough, and resilient enough to manage whatever life brings. No one is born with all the answers, you become the answers along the way.
—Cyndi Lynne, www.cyndilynne.com

You're going to remember 2 powerful messages from 2 powerful women in your life. Those 2 women: your Mama and your Granny. You'll always need to remember this from your Mama: nothing beats a failure, but a try. This will help you to always face your fears and forever pursue your dreams. The second from Granny, two whole words that literally sound like a lifetime: keep livin'. Tanya, remember these words of these infamously, powerful, insightful women; they've changed your life and will continue to do so, even when they're gone their legacy stands.
—Tanya J. Miller, www.tanyajmiller.com

Continue to discover who you are, what you care about, and what lights your fire. Ideas, desires, and beliefs change through time. It is not about a job or a career, but a life well-lived. Amazing opportunities will continue to present themselves when you live your truth. Believe strongly in your philosophy: Eat Real

Food, Make Good Decisions, and Be Accountable as
it has always kept you on track to live your personal
Healthy, Happy Lifestyle and support others who
desire Health and happiness on their terms.
—*Denise Stegall, www.livinghealthylist.com*

My Future Self is NOW. The Eternal Now is your
future self; the future of love is now; the self and love,
and love of self, and future is now. The past has been
released and loved free. And the future is nothing more
than the continuation of today, this sacred NOW. This
sacred moment is all there is; Bring your future self
into the "Now" and into the next "Now." Time keeps on
slipping into the Now! My Future Self is NOW.
—*Kornelia Stephanie, https://korneliastephanie.com*

The most important thing I've noticed I haven't learned
to do is put "me" first. Not selfishly, not rudely, not with
judgment but lovingly and with care for me to realize
I'm so important I need to take care of my "full self"
first so I can be my best for others. If you read this and
haven't yet learned self-care, stop everything, and take a
course, do a self-study, find a coach to teach and support
you. Without us taking care of ourselves, we are not our
best for others. The love it takes to find time to meditate,
do breathing, be healthy with food and physical activity,
and have space to vision, manifest, and write is essential.
Love me enough to do that.
—*Laura Bly, Consciously Growing*

What's meant for you won't pass you by. Even in times of trial, there are benevolent forces more powerful than you can imagine at work on your behalf. You are protected from snares large and small, that are deflected before they can even reach your field of vision. So, carve out your path in the peace of knowing you are upheld by the everlasting arms.

—Evie Lennon, Author of Drawing Comfort for Chronic Conditions

Your greatest challenges will teach you compassion and empathy for others. You are more resilient than you know, and your experiences will help to change lives.

—Tonia Ahern

Trust yourself. Remember who you are and what YOU want. It's ok to BE happy, to BE grateful, to BE YOU. Nurture your soul. Keep giving from your heart. Through God's grace, your gifts will never diminish.

—Yvonne L. St. Andrew, @ylsvaservices.com

Here is YOUR opportunity to speak to your Future Self:

WITH SUCH GRATITUDE

Thanks to Sibyl English. Here is it, Sibyl! My third book in my *soul-connection series*, anthologies from my articles in Sibella Publications International. Thank you for your continued encouragement and support of my writing.

Nechama Laber, Publisher, JGU Press. Thank you for your partnership. *I am delighted to let readers know that 100% of the proceeds from my soul-connection series books support the organization we co-founded, Jewish Girls Unite, found here: jewishgirlsunite.com.*

Leah Caras, of Carasmatic Design, book designer extraordinaire. I can't say enough how delighted I am with your book design, thank you!

Yvonne L. St. Andrew, my Virtual Assistant. Thank you for all you do to keep me on track! Thank you for the part you played getting this book back on track.

To the 'sisters' who played along in my Dear Future Self game, giving thought, and sharing their quotes for inspiration in this book: Tonia Ahern, Judy Bloomberg, Susan Cohen, Abigail Goldberg Spiegel, Alina Haitz, Evie Lennon, Laura Lowenthal Bly, Cyndi Lynne

Lamarucciola, Tanya J. Miller, Yvonne L. St. Andrew, Denise Stegall, Kornelia Stephanie – thank you all!

To my cherished clients, I love you! I'm grateful to you and for you. YOU helped me find my future self!

Finally, to my family members and dear sister-friends, you have supported me on my journey through challenges and obstacles I thought I might not be able to overcome. Yet here I am. Because of you. *Dear Future Self...continue to say Yes when someone offers to help!*

For Rebecca and Sarah, XXOOM

ABOUT THE AUTHOR

Susan Axelrod, CCP, TIPC is the go-to Confidence Coach for Women. Specializing in working with executive women and matriarchs in mid-life who have spent decades doing for others and are now starting businesses or other personal endeavors in their 'second half.' Using co-creative & co-facilitative coaching methods, Susan helps clients uncover the inspired soul within who is looking to live out life in a self-fulfilling and purposeful way. Susan doesn't give answers or advice. She works with clients to dig into their core, to explore the girl she was and the woman she wants to be for the rest of her life, personally, professionally, spiritually, and physically. Using original Confident-Life™ Tools, Susan helps women find the Clarity and Confidence they seek to live out a *Best Life*. She works with women in transition who declare themselves 'READY!' …ready to GROW, ready to LIVE now and create a meaningful legacy. Susan's contagious enthusiasm and deep listening skills sparks and motivates clients to get Confident and Thrive! Susan also works with women in business for themselves and small business owners, teaching her Intuitive Business System™, the system with which she has grown her own successful fulltime coaching business. Susan is an Influencer in the KS MEDIA APP. Get inspired for your Future Self by downloading the app now!

Looking for Motivational Speaking or Workshops?

Susan's Confident-Life Workshops™ and speaking engagements are a hit every time! Available for work-teams, book clubs, friend groups, women CEO clubs, nonprofits or any place women gather. Using Tai Chi and Qigong as a basis to connect to Self, Susan weaves mindfulness and conscious awareness into everything she does.

Certifications:

- Certified Coach Practitioner, through The Coach Training Academy [accredited by the International Coaching Federation and Certified Coaches Alliance].
- Trauma Informed Professional Coach, certified through Lodestar.
- Qigong & Tai Chi Easy Teacher, certified by the Institute of Integral Qigong & Tai Chi.

Other Books - Available on Amazon:

100% of the proceeds from these books support the global organization co-founded by the author, Jewish Girls Unite jewishgirlsunite.com

ARE YOU READY TO LIVE A MORE CONFIDENT-LIFE™?

Contact Susan now, you'll be glad you did.

When you call, Susan responds. Everything is timely, 100% personal, and 100% custom. Connect personally now for coaching, or to bring a Confident-Life Workshop™ or Motivational Speaker to your group. Learn about Susan and her work here: www.whatwillyourlegacybe.com.

CONTACT: susan@confident-life.com | 518-495-4573